SOMERSET AT WORK
1870 to 1950
Joan Astell

REDCLIFFE
Bristol

First published in 1986 by
Redcliffe Press Ltd, 49 Park Street, Bristol 1

© Joan Astell 1986

ISBN 0 948265 60 4

*Typeset and printed in Great Britain by
Penwell Ltd, Parkwood, Callington, Cornwall*

ABOUT THIS BOOK

This is Joan Astell's second book in the *Somerset Heritage Series*. Her first title *Somerset Scrapbook 1920-1940* concentrated on the pioneering work of one photographer, the remarkable Alfred Vowles. However, for this book she has scoured the museums and company archives throughout the county, as well as utilising her own unique collection. One of her prime aims was to select images that had rarely been used before. In so many books about Somerset, the same familiar photographs are recycled again and again. Of the 101 photographs in *Somerset at Work* only a handful have ever been published in books before. Moments of festivity and 'play' have been included among the 'work' pictures and the book adds up to a surprising, revealing and important record of people's lives throughout the whole county.

ACKNOWLEDGEMENTS

The author and publishers would like to thank all the museums, companies and individuals who have given generously of their time and resources.

Admiral Blake Museum, Bridgwater: 7 (bottom), 47 (bottom), 48 (top), 60 (top and bottom). Glastonbury Rural Life Museum: 32 (top and bottom), 33, 41 (bottom), 46 (top). Wellington Museum: 8 (top), 18 (top), 19 (left and right), 26 (top and bottom), 27 (bottom), 42 (top and bottom), 52 (bottom). Wells Museum: 25 (top), 38 (top and bottom), 43 (top), 44, 46 (bottom), 47 (top), 54 (bottom), 55 (top and bottom). West Somerset Museum, Allerford: 4, 5, 6 (top and bottom), 10 (top and bottom), 14 (top and bottom), 28 (bottom), 31 (top), 45. Woodspring Museum: 40 (top), 48 (bottom). Yeovil Museum: 24 (top and bottom), 27 (top), 36, 37 (top), 50 (top), 52 (top), 53 (top). C & J Clark Archive, Street: 21, 22 (top and bottom), 41 (top), 43 (bottom). National Film Archive/Thorn EMI Screen Entertainment: 58, 59 (top). J W Singer & Sons, Frome: 15, 16, 17. Swaynes, Bridgwater/Burnham/ Minehead: 23 (top and bottom). Taunton Cider Company: 34, 35 (top and bottom). John Cornwall: 12 (top and bottom), 13. Jack Floyde: 50 (bottom), 61. Joan Astell Collection: 29, 30 (top and bottom), 31 (bottom), 39 (top and bottom), 40 (bottom), 49 (top and bottom), 51 (top and bottom), 54 (top), 56 (top and bottom), 57 (top and bottom), 59 (bottom), 61 (bottom).

SHRIMPS AND EELS

The River Parrett, along with the Axe and the Brue discharges into
Bridgwater Bay and it is along this weird coast that one finds todays
unknown Somerset in spite of, or perhaps because of, its complete domination
by the building and power lines of the Hinkley Point Nuclear Power Station.
The visitor today, as he surveys this flat windswept landscape crossed with
rhynes (a large ditch or drain) and high causies (causeways) just wide enough
to permit the passage of a single car, will find little evidence of the shrimp and

eel catching of the photographs, once the major industry of the district. Huge pebble barriers protect the Steart Island Bird Sanctuary from inundation but where the villages once joined the sea, now there is dereliction and the net poles seem to have been abandoned along with the cottages. Further inland the village of Stolford, with its wooden church of St Peter, looks bright and tidy, a bonus from the employment brought by the power station.

Kilve a little further down the coast on the other side of the power station has a strange paved effect to its beach and it is between the slabs that the eels lurked. Today it is less lonely than Stolford for the large car park and agreeable ruins bring large numbers of visitors to stroll along an almost unspoilt coast.

Below: KILVE. Eel fishing was known as glatting, a term rarely heard today. The fisherman holds the 'eel-spear' in his left hand.

Opposite: BRIDG-
WATER BAY. Shrimping
at Stolford. The curious
sledge (*below*) was pushed
over the muddy bay to the
nets and was known as a
'mud-horse'.

Above: MINEHEAD.
Once a working
harbour. In 1701 it
could boast 30 ships
totalling 1084 tons
manned by 137
seamen. Here in 1870
one can see the large
coastal traders still but
by 1894 there were
only 10 local vessels
and trade continued to
decline steadily.
Left: BRIDG-
WATER. The exact
purpose of the dive is
not known but the pre-
war pioneering
equipment used is of
exceptional interest.

Above: MINEHEAD. A yachting cup is proudly displayed outside the Pier hotel. Could these boats really have been raced in the harbour, the waters of which have spelt doom to many larger craft? c1910.

Right: PORLOCK. Increasingly, all along the coast, pleasure craft were taking the place of the working boats. 1939.

Opposite above: WELLINGTON. The residents celebrate Lifeboat Day 1908 with someone else's lifeboat. This was eventually launched at the Basins, constructed to store water to power a woollen mill.

Opposite below: MINEHEAD — LIFEBOAT DAY 1926. The boat is believed to be the George Leicester manned by 12 men with sails and oars. In service from 1901 to 1927.

CANALS: The late 1940s—the lock staircase and the coal wharf lay rotting, overtaken by the railway and the road. Kennet & Avon and Somersetshire Coal Canal.

COAL AND CANALS

It is hard for the visitor to realise that Somerset once had a thriving coalmining area, primarily based round the villages of Radstock, Midsomer Norton and Camerton. In 1681 pits in this area produced 100,000 tons per annum.

Even so, much of the consumption was local, not reaching as far as Bristol and with the coming of the canals to South Wales in 1792 a short cheap sea journey could bring their superior coal into Bristol, thus rendering possible expansion with improved transport hardly worth seeking.

Despite this entrepreneurs could see improved markets for Somerset coal if canals could be built to carry it away. This was the time of canal mania and Somerset joined in to the full, spawning the Kennet and Avon (1794) together with many more schemes that came to little or nothing. For the Somersetshire Coal Canal they built locks, aqueducts, tunnels, caissons, weighbridges and wharves.

The canals prospered for a time but the railways soon threatened and by the 1870s they had won. The Somerset Coal Canal was wound up in 1893 and finally abandoned in 1904 when the GWR constructed the Camerton to Limpley Stoke railway on its course. By 1966 the railways too had gone to be followed only a few years later by the last of the coalmines. It was the close of an era when, for a while, Somerset was simultaneously mining coal around Radstock, lead in the Mendips and iron ore in the Brendon Hills.

Below: MENDIP LEAD MINING. These hills above Cheddar have been worked for lead for over 2,000 years. Here are old mine entrances.

Above: RADSTOCK: Writhlington Colliery c1910.
Opposite top: Early breathing apparatus, c1910.
Opposite bottom: Underground workers in Newbury Colliery with candle holders in their caps. Underground manager is on the left, with an unusual style of lamp.

Above:
SEDGEMOOR. Although its use has changed from a household fuel to an aid to gardening, peat is still dug on these often-flooded levels.

Right: KILVE. The memory of what might have been. In 1920 this tiny hamlet looked like being the centre of an oil bonanza. This oil retort house was built to exploit its areas of oil bearing shales—but it all came to nothing. Picture c1948.

FROME. John Webb Singer, founder of the firm.

THE FOUNDRY—FROME

Originally like so many other towns in the county Frome produced cloth and had done since time immemorial. John Webb Singer was not even in its traditional industry, he was by trade a clockmaker with, until 1849, a business in Eagle Lane. Requested by his vicar to make a pair of candlesticks for St John's Church this keen churchman willingly complied. So exquisite was the workmanship that other orders poured in and soon the firm was producing altar crosses, sanctuary lamps, eagle lecterns etc.

These were followed by requests for life size statues to such an extent that he had to import foreign labour to produce them. Four Belgians he brought over came with their secret wax moulding process for small models.

Gradually Singer's bronze work spread throughout the country; Boadicea on Westminster Bridge, Peter Pan in Kensington Gardens, the Burghers of Calais, the Chancel Screen at Westminster Cathedral, The Dome and Balustrading at the Central Hall Westminster, General Gordon seated on a camel (for which a special high roofed workshop had to be built), Justice over the Old Bailey and the giant King Alfred that commands the main street of Winchester.

During the first world war the foundry turned over to munitions but at its end the demand for war memorials kept them busy for the next nine years. These included the Shanghai Memorial and the Memorial of Scotland at Edinburgh Castle on which every branch of the services is depicted down to the minutest details of the carrier pigeon and canary.

Over the years, with amalgamations the product changed to hot brass pressings and pressure diecasting but it sits still in the very centre of the little town totally at home with its more ancient surroundings.

Above: FROME. J W Singer's bronze foundry prior to 1902. Among the patriotic Queen Victorias a benign lion warms his back against the stove. that Tennyson's head on the table?

Opposite: FROME. 4 tons of Welsh lion is prepared for a lifetime on top of the dome of Cardiff Town Hall at the foundry of J W Singer.

Above: WELLINGTON. Bishop Brothers foundry. "Plumbers, Gasfitters, Bellhangers, manufacturers of Bishop's Improved Kitchen Range fitted with boilers for supplying Baths and Hot Water to any part of the house. Hot water Apparatus for heating Churches, Chapels, Greenhouses, Halls etc."

Right: BRIDGWATER. The cement works. 1928.

Above: WELLINGTON. The tower of All Saints, Rockwell Green being added to take the spire.
Left: TAUNTON. The spire of All Saints, Rockwell Green, Wellington being built at Moggridge's in 1908.

LEATHER AND CLOTH

In every part of Somerset there is evidence of the past manufacture of both leather and cloth and although both must have had their origins in the abundance of good grazing for sheep and cattle, by as early as the 16th Century skins were being imported from Spain and only dressed here, whilst the harbour records of Minehead show that both wool and cloth were being imported during the reign of Elizabeth I.

Towns tended to specialise, hence the shoes and sheepskin products of Street and the gloves of Yeovil. Tanning and dressing the skins was countywide and with the importing starting so early it is not surprising to find a large tannery at Minehead which, in the days before tourism, made much of its wealth from its harbour.

Below: MINEHEAD. The tanyard in 1906. Until 1934, when demolished to make way for a cinema, this was Minehead's largest single industry. Management are seated whilst the foreman dominates the back row.

The glove trade in Yeovil began as an offshoot of the parchment industry which inevitably suffered considerable setbacks with the mass production of paper, although as Yeovil also made linen the impact was lessened. It is the size of the glove trade that was so staggering. In 1834 they produced 1,800,000 pairs and the number of people, including children, employed was 20,000—most houses having at least one outworker. All this was before the introduction of the sewing machine.

Cloth in the form of woollens, sailcloths and linens was everywhere but trade now has all but ceased leaving Wellington with the only firm still making cloth in any quantity.

Below: STREET. The cluttered workshop of the Shoemaker. 1894.

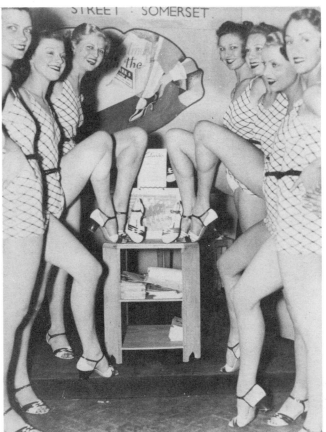

Above: STREET. 1893 the trimming room employees, Clarks Shoes. How demure these rather young workers look holding their flowers. The zip fastener had yet to be invented hence the profusion of pearl buttons.
Left and below: STREET. 1935 C B Cochrane's Young Ladies model Clark's Colarado sandals at the Health and Beauty Exhibition in London.

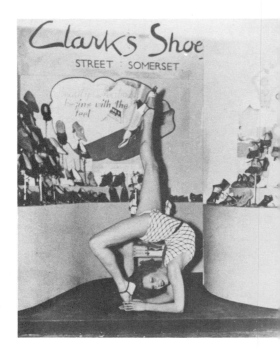

Above: BRIDGWATER. Carnival has a long standing tradition in Somerset and Bridgwater leads the way. Business and societies vie with each other to produce the best floats. Here is Swaynes Shoe Repairers' float in the early 50s.

Right: BRIDGWATER. Shoes, however good, wear down and this repair workshop of the early 50s contrasts greatly with the 'while you wait' shops of today.

Above: YEOVIL. The machine shop of Thring and Luffman's Reckleford Glove Factory. No electric power for the machines yet, they are treadle worked. *Left:* YEOVIL. Leather workers in the 1920s. Glove manufacture appears in the town's history from 1327.

Above: WELLS. The remains of the wool trade. Machinery lies idle awaiting times that will not return. c1935.
Right: SPAXTON. The village church has this mediaeval bench end depicting the wool trade. The fuller at work with the tools of his trade above him.

Above: WELLINGTON. Fox Brothers Steam Waggon with trailer in 1897. This firm continued the woollen industry that had been in Wellington perhaps as far back as 1357.

Below: WELLINGTON. Around 1896 Fox Brothers discovered the true shade of khaki (a secret still held by the firm) and produced puttees (cloth leggings) for the Boer War. During the first world war they were turning out 70,000 pairs a week.

Above: YEOVIL. The recruiting parade 1914/18 war. The leading soldier wears the puttees made in Wellington.
Right: Factory children at Fox's with the puttees during the 1st World War.

Above: ALCOMBE. Sheep dipping. "The best thing about sheep dipping was when one of the men fell in".
Opposite: NORTH CURRY. The gardener at Moredon with his wife. In the 1890s in addition to the large grounds the house supported three large heated conservatories.
Below: DUNSTER. The watermill. By the temporary roof this picture would seem to have been taken in 1946 when it was described in L F Holme's *Dunster: an English Village* as being 'newly restored'. Note the unusual double wheels.

Above: ATHELNEY DISTRICT. Withies drying by the road on the Somerset Levels, the last remains of the basket-makers trade.

Right: SELWORTHY. Even when this picture was taken thatching was becoming a vanishing trade, but the existence of this village will insure that it never dies completely.

Opposite: The shadows lengthen as horse and master leave the fields with the hay. The idyllic traditional picture of work in Somerset now little more than a memory.

Above: QUANTOCK HILLS. Whortleberry Pickers.
Picking 'worts' was such a major industry that schools
closed because so many of the children were on the hills.
They still grow in profusion but their popularity has waned.
Opposite top: CHEDDAR. Making the strawberry baskets.
Opposite bottom: CHEDDAR. The now filled baskets leave
by special train for the big city markets. This area is known
countrywide for its cheese and caves but few know that
even today it produces a very fair strawberry.

CIDER

Even in living memory each village and in earlier times each street, had its own press and cider house. Now the home brew seems confined to farms and the popular market has been claimed by two large firms. Depsite this some of the old cider customs linger—the wassail is still celebrated at The Butchers Arms, Carhampton, Nr Minehead on 17 January each year when the apples are serenaded, toast left for the robin and guns fired to scare off the evil spirits. Taunton still chooses a Cider Queen to reign over the apple harvest.

Recent market research revealed that consumers' conception of cider ranged from 'pop' to strong drink, sometimes referred to as 'mad man's broth' and everyone knows how many downfalls have been attributed to over-imbibing of scrumpy, that cloudy greenish brew which mocks the unwary to under-estimate its strength. Indeed the last persons to be publicly hanged in North Somerset in 1830—William Wall a cider house keeper, James Rowley and Richard Clarke, who met their maker in a field at Kenn near Nailsea watched by an audience of 15,000—all blamed cider for their ruin although the notice over the gallows read 'For Rick Burning'.

Cider production was started in Norton Fitzwarren in 1911 and evolved to become a company which produces an incredible 19 million gallons per year.

Below: NORTON FITZWARREN. Taunton Cider delivery van. It was based on the Model T Ford and had pneumatic tyres on the front but solid on the back with wooden wheels.

Right: NORTON FITZWARREN. Joe Mustell the head cooper at Taunton Cider. He retired in the late 1940s after a lifetime with the company.
Below: NORTON FITZWARREN. Cider barrels being loaded at the main entrance of Taunton Cider in 1930.

YEOVIL'S AIRCRAFT INDUSTRY

Below: YEOVIL. James Petter with twins Percy and Ernest in the back, steering the car powered by an engine designed and built by themselves at the orignal factory at Huish.

Somerset is not famed for heavy industry but Yeovil found fame from it. In 1895 James B Petter a local ironmonger designed a small car. His factory, already producing Nautilus fire grates, soon expanded to make Petter Oil engines. At the outbreak of the First World war the entire resources of Petters was placed at the disposal of the government and Sir Ernest Petter built a new factory at Westland where Short 184 Float Planes were made.

Amalgamation in 1939 caused the closure of the Yeovil foundry and Nautilus works, but the Westland Aircraft Group continues building aircraft and between the wars produced the 'Seafire' and 'Lysander' and the tail-less 'Pterodactyl', a famous experimental aeroplane. Subsequently helicopters dominated the scene.

Above: YEOVIL. Women workers at Westlands during the 1914/18 war.
Below: MINEHEAD. M. Salmet lands on the sands. It is said locally that members of Minehead Council were given a trial flight but things went wrong and they came down in the sea, wet but unhurt.

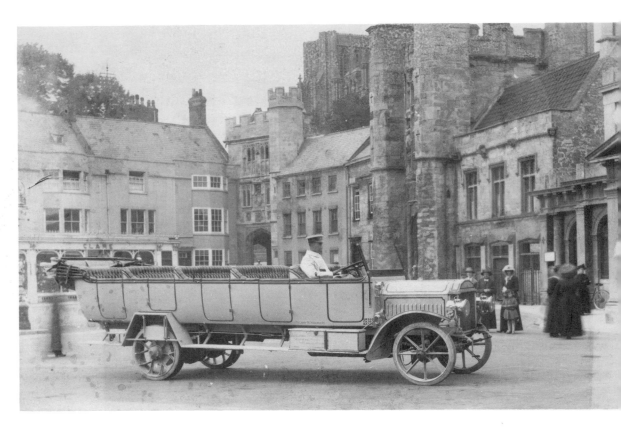

Above: COUNTY GATE. The Minehead to Lynmouth bus in January, 1937. It had started from Minehead on Thursday but the last passengers only reached their destinations on Monday. The hospitality of a nearby cottage ensured they survived the ordeal.

Right: DULVERTON. The Rural District Council's assistant surveyor (leaning against the car) poses with the diggers as the brow of the hill is achieved. 1929.

Opposite top: WELLS. The Bristol Tramways & Carriage Co's bus waits by the Penniless Porch, Market Place, Wells. Despite the length of the coach it only held eighteen passengers in its button back leather upholstered benches. 1915.

Opposite bottom: WELLS. Jewell's Garage Priory Road, believed to be the first garage in that town. The two cars are taxis and the bus is a charabanc for hire. Around 1920.

Above: WESTON SUPER MARE. A ten
minute service ran along the seafront,
which between its start in 1902 and demise
in 1937 carried 51 million passengers.
These summer open-sided trams were
nicknamed 'toast racks'.

Right: COMBE ROW. The iron ore mines
of the Brendon Hills gave rise to the
construction of a mineral railway to carry
the ore down to the docks at Watchet.
Despite the somewhat primitive seating
arrangements quite a good passenger
traffic built up. 1894.

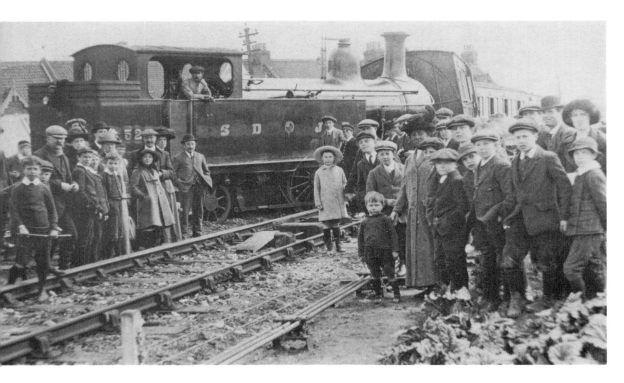

Above: BURNHAM ON SEA. Easter 1914 the Clarks excursion train is derailed entering Burnham Station. The engine driver looks unpeturbed by the mess.
Below: GLASTONBURY. Market Street. 1930. With the onlookers beautifully arranged in height order.

Above: WELLINGTON. The bicycle club assemble at Courtland Road Girls School in 1888. The range of early cycles here repays close study.

Left: WELLINGTON. John Reynold Miller, manager of Stuckey's Bank, Wellington on his boneshaker.

Opposite top: BUTLEIGH. The steam roller and tar cart belonging to Robert Neville at work in Wells during the 1930s. The squire of the village had a passion for engines and owned one of the first cars in the country.

Opposite bottom: STREET. Berliet Travellers Car (20mph). Specially built for Clarks of Street it enabled the representative to show his samples easily to the client right outside the premises. 1921.

SHEPTON MALLET. The travelling ironmonger. c1900.

TAUNTON. The knife grinder, once a familiar sight in town and village.

Above: GLASTONBURY. Tom Syms the mobile fish and chip man. See the guillotine chip cutter on the far side of the cart. c1900.

Below: WELLS. Doorstep delivery by churn or bottle just before World War 2. These wide necked bottles had cardboard tops in which there was a small perforated circle. This could be pushed out to facilitate getting the whole top off or used to put a straw through.

Above: WELLS. High Street, Wells around 1900. The staff of the India and China Tea Company pose for their picture.
Right: BRIDG-WATER. A picture to justify the claim that women's work is never done. Happily the picture was taken shortly before the demolition of the property in a slum clearance plan. Wash-house at No 7 Court, Albert Street, Bridgwater.

Above: A day by the sea was not the prerogative of the working classes. Here the Barrett family of North Curry pays hommage to Beechams Pills.

Right: NORTH CURRY. The Barrett family at Moredon on holiday.

Opposite top: BRIDGWATER. A wet and windy official opening of the Bridgwater swimming baths on 21 August 1893.

Opposite bottom: WESTON SUPER MARE. Sand sculpture around 1909 believed to depict the Boer War. These works, built just below the promenade so that coins could be thrown to them by the visitors, were terrible tear jerkers. This is 'The Last Message' which was obviously fatal to both horses and soldier.

Above: YEOVIL. The 1914 Marathon. An event seemingly totally shunned by the female population, not even an encouraging presence.

Below: DUNSTER. 1925. "After a visit extending over two months His Highness the Maharajah of Jodpur most generously presented the West Somerset Polo Club with a well-fitted and up to date pavilion to replace the one previously used." West Somerset Polo Club Handbook 1936.

Above: DUNSTER. Around 1910 and the village awaits the arrival of the hunt.
Below: NORTH CURRY. These dogs would have been used for fox or hare hunting. The strange barrels are kennels for dogs to be kept away from the pack—a bitch with puppies or similar. 1890s.

Above: YEOVIL. 1887 Jubilee. Lizzie Little wins the Donkey Derby.

Opposite top: YEOVIL. Nearly every village possessed a "brassen band" whatever else it lacked in social amenity.

Opposite bottom: BRIDGWATER. The Choral Society 1898. Despite a good display of quite tropical plants the outdoor clothing of the singers hints that the heating of the Town Hall left something to be desired.

Below: DUNSTER. As if the people of Dunster hadn't seen enough of their Yarn Market! A replica at the fête in the castle grounds is outshone by the popularity of the tea tent just about to open in the foreground. 1925.

Left: EXMOOR, DUNKERY BEACON. Ready to be fired for the coronation of King George V in 1911.
Below: WELLS. Carnival 1902. The bonfire poses with its builders.

Above: WELLS. The Fire Brigade ready for the parade to mark the coronation of Edward VII in 1902.

Below: WELLS. Holloway and Clares of the Market Place decorate for the Jubilee.

Above: NORTH CURRY. Two young ladies playing with their dolls.
Right: NORTH CURRY. Young Master Barrett looks slightly uncomfortable when cast in the rôle of Sir Francis Drake.
Opposite top: NORTH CURRY. The beautiful trees of Moredon give background to this rather strange smoking party. They appear to have neither tobacco or matches and none of the pipes is alight. c1900.
Opposite bottom: NORTH CURRY. The intrepid tobogganers of Moredon. c1900.

FILM MAKING

Although Somerset can boast no locally based film companies, use of the scenery has been going on, both amateur and professional, since the first movie camera turned.

There is, however, one story that has to date been filmed six times, many of them using the Exmoor locations so that now many visitors to these places cannot be convinced that the story of *Lorna Doone* is really fictional.

The first film of this classic tale by R D Blackmore was made in 1912 and starred Dorothy Bellew as Lorna. Another British silent version with Bertie Gordon and Dennis Wyndham as Lorna and Jan followed in 1920 and close on the heels of this came the American attempt, with Madge Bellamy in the title rôle (1922).

All these, of course, had been silent but in 1935 came the start of the talkie versions from which the illustrations are taken. Its re-issue in 1949 brought renewed interest in the story and the Americans had another go in 1951 with Barbara Hale and Richard Greene.

The fall in popularity of the cinema brought no such fall for Lorna and in 1960 BBC television made it yet again.

Of the many other films using Somerset as a background do you remember—The Farmer's Wife (Timberscombe 1929), The Ghost Train (Camerton 1935), The Lone Scout and The Trail of Youth (Minehead 1935), Kate Plus 10 (Dunkerton Colliery sidings 1937), Titchfield Thunderbolt (1952 Monkton Combe), The Last Visitor (1981 TV Minehead), The Invisible Man (1982 TV Minehead and Luccombe)? The list could go on and on.

58

Above and opposite: EXMOOR. The shooting of Lorna Doone. 1935 saw the first talking version being made on location. It starred Victoria Hopper and John Loder as Lorna and Jan with some local people also taking part. It was re-issued in 1949.

Below: MINEHEAD. The celebrated *Lorna Doone* coach makes a fun run between Minehead and Lynton. It stands outside the now demolished "Plume of Feathers" coaching inn at Minehead. Extra horses and passenger power were frequently required to get it up Porlock Hill. c1950.

Above: BRIDGWATER. The old borough police force. Twelve policemen for a town the size of Bridgwater seems to show particularly law abiding inhabitants.
Below: BRIDGWATER. First sitting of the Borough Petty Sessions, Court House, North Gate. 3 February 1913.

Above: MINEHEAD. 1920. The Rat Catchers—twopence a tail from the council.

Below: NORTH CURRY. The staff of the High Sherriff of Somerset, William Barrett assemble in the grounds of Moredon. 1892. It is believed that the photographer was Mr Barrett himself.

SOMERSET SCRAPBOOK 1920 to 1940   Joan Astell   £2.95

Joan Astell's first book is an acclaimed collection of photographs of West Somerset which takes us back to a world, still within living memory but today changed beyond belief. It is a world of quiet roads, lonely farms and isolated villages; of pre-mechanised farming and flourishing country crafts. It is a time when holidaymakers arrived at the county's resorts by rail excursion or charabanc, to watch pierrot shows on the sea-front.

To present this vanished Somerset, Joan Astell has drawn on her superb collection of photographs taken by the remarkable Alfred Vowles. From just before the first world war until shortly after the second, Alfred Vowles observed and recorded, the county he passionately loved.

SCENES FROM A SOMERSET CHILDHOOD   Llewelyn Powys   £3.95

This book presents a unique collection of images, both verbal and visual, of life in a small Somerset community at the turn of the century.

Llewelyn Powys was born in Dorchester in 1884 but was only 18 months old when his father became vicar of Montacute and the family moved to the Somerset village which was to be the centre of his life for the next 29 years.

These were years of great happiness, and Llewelyn would frequently spend his days exploring the surrounding countryside with his brothers and sisters.

Lyrical, often inspiring, descriptions of people and places remembered from childhood are complemented by a superb selection of period photographs of the village and surrounding area in which Llewelyn Powys grew up.

Through his distinctive, carefully-fashioned and yet seemingly carefree prose, the author draws us back, as if by magic, into the innocent world he shared with his family before the mechanics of modern civilisation began to transform life in this most beautiful and remote of England's counties.

Other Books of West Country interest

Redcliffe Press are the leading publishers of books on Somerset and Avon, with more in course of preparation.

The following is a selection of our West Country titles:

Somerset & Avon Ghosts, Witches and Legends by
John Bailey £1.95

Journalist John Bailey graphically retells the stories of 27 mysterious happenings. From the macabre resurrection of a 16th century corpse to ghostly sightings by motorists on the A370 at Congresbury, all are treated with an entertaining mixture of journalistic scepticism and wry humour.

Old Somerset Customs by Muriel Walker £1.95

Somerset is rich in ancient customs, folklore and superstitions. Collop Monday, the Tatworth candle auction, the Minehead hobbyhorse, orchard wassailing . . . these and many more Somerset customs are brought vividly to life in a collection which will delight residents and visitor alike.

Weston-Super-Mare: Good Old Days by John Bailey £1.95

Who better to tell the story of the famous seaside resort than the man who edited the *Weston Mercury* for twenty years? Packed with fascinating and amusing anecdotes and over 50 nostalgic photographs.

Sacred & Satiric by J.H. Bettey and C.W.G. Taylor £2.25

The story of the stone carvings in West Country churches—their subjects ranging from the deeply religious to the monstrous and grotesque.

Profusely illustrated from churches in Somerset, Avon, Gloucestershire and Wiltshire.

Bath by Edith Sitwell hardback £8.95

At last—a new edition of the celebrated study of eighteenth century social life in Bath. Captures the atmosphere of the times superbly, with Beau Nash and all the famous personalities who graced the period with their wit, their beauty and their eccentricity.

The illustrations include Rowlandson's 'Comforts of Bath'.

Bath: Profile of a City by Paul Hardy and William Lowndes
£4.95

Superb drawings of many of Bath's finest buildings, and some lesser known gems, with brilliant 'pen portraits' giving the stories of the people who lived there.

Dorset Essays by Llewelyn Powys hardback £6.95

An evocation of the Dorset countryside and its people in the early years of this century, by a modern master of English prose writing. Photographs by Ann Clarke.

Thirteen Worthies By Llewelyn Powys £2.50

From Chaucer to Hardy, a collection of delightful vignettes of men whose lives the author found admirable and interesting—including the Dorset poet William Barnes, and Tom Coryat, born in the Somerset village of Odcombe in 1577 and later to be the eccentric chronicler of travels on foot in Europe and Asia.

Skin for Skin by Llewelyn Powys £1.75

First published in 1926, this West Country classic recalls life in the Edwardian era. Chapters on Montacute, the Dorset and Somerset countryside, a stay with brother T.F Powys in the village of East Chaldon and recollections of Christmas and New Year's Eve.

Earth Memories by Llewelyn Powys hardback £6.95

This collection contains many of Powys' finest country essays, including 'The Other Side of the Quantocks' and the author's first visit, in search of family memories, to the Dorset village of Stalbridge. With introduction by Philip Larkin.

West Country Stone Walls by Janet Bodman £1.35

A unique county-by-county survey of the stones, patterns and techniques used for centuries by craftsmen building in natural stone, from Bristol to Land's End.

 The 12 colour photographs (and 14 in black and white) complement the author's descriptions of the many beautiful colours to be found in some of the walls.

Wookey: The Caves Beyond by Martin Farr £1.50

The gripping story of cave diving at Wookey Hole. The author is a noted diver himself, as well as being an internationally famed underwater photographer.

Please ask your bookseller about any of these books. In case of difficulty, they may be obtained direct from Redcliffe Press Ltd., 49 Park Street, Bristol BS1 5NT, enclosing your cheque. Please add carriage of 75p for order up to £5, and £1 on orders over £5.

A catalogue of our full list of West Country titles is also available.